BUILDING
Science Skills

by
Barbara J. Fagenbaum

**Cover Design by
Jannette Bole**

Published by Instructional Fair · TS Denison
an imprint of

About the Author

Barbara J. Fagenbaum currently teaches second grade at the Charter School of Science and Technology in Rochester, New York. Her experience as a science instructor has been with students in public school and science museum settings. She received an A.A.S. degree in medical technology from Rochester Institute of Technology, a B.S. degree in psychology from Nazareth College of Rochester, and an M.S. degree in elementary education from the State University of New York at Brockport. Her interest in science began as a young girl while trying to prove she was smarter than her big brother. She is also the author of *Science: Girls Allowed and Boys, Too!* also published by McGraw-Hill Children's Publishing.

Credits

Author: Barbara J. Fagenbaum
Cover Design: Jannette Bole, Matthew Van Zomeren
Project Director/Editor: Debra Olson Pressnall
Editors: Mary Rose Hassinger, Sara Bierling, Kate Wheeler
Graphic Design and Layout: Jannette Bole
Cover Photos: Artville, Digital Stock

McGraw-Hill
Children's Publishing
A Division of The McGraw-Hill Companies

Published by Instructional Fair • TS Denison
An imprint of McGraw-Hill Children's Publishing
Copyright © 2002 McGraw-Hill Children's Publishing

Limited Reproduction Permission: Permission to duplicate these materials is limited to the person for whom they are purchased. Reproduction for an entire school or school district is unlawful and strictly prohibited.

Send all inquiries to:

McGraw-Hill Children's Publishing
3195 Wilson Drive NW
Grand Rapids, Michigan 49544

All Rights Reserved • Printed in the United States of America

Building Science Skills
ISBN: 0-7424-0251-7

1 2 3 4 5 6 7 8 9 07 06 05 04 03 02

Table of Contents

Introduction 4
Scientific Method Terminology 5

Whole Class Experiments 6
Model Student Lab Sheet 7
What's in a Name? 8
Popcorn Party 12
Math Test—Hard or Easy? 16
Silence Is Golden 23
Iced Batteries 31
Let It Grow! Let It Grow! 35
How Long Will It Go? 40

Individual or Small Group Experiments 45
Student Lab Sheet 46
Do Sneakers Help You Jump Higher? 49
How Does What a Cup Is Made of Affect Insulation? 50
How Does Acid Rain Affect Grass Growth? 52
How Does Physical Exercise Affect Reaction Time? 54
How Does Weight Affect the Flight of a Paper Airplane? 56
How Does Color of Food Affect Preference? 58
What Color Clothing Keeps You Warmest? 59
What Could Be Added to Bubble Solution to Make the Bubbles Last Longer? ... 60
How Does Size Affect the Dissolving Rate of Sugar in Water? 63
What Is the Effect of Fertilizer on Grass Growth? 64
What Is the Effect of Music on Memory? 66
How Does Exercise Affect Lung Capacity? 69
Assessment Rubric 70

Culminating Event—A Science Fair 71
Planning Checklist for Teacher 72
Guidelines for Science Fair Display 73
Science Fair Investigation Checklist 74
Science Fair Display Checklist 75
Experiment Possibilities 76
Judging Rubric 78
Participation Certificate 79
Participation Ribbons 80

Introduction

The scientific method is a foundational experimental approach used informally by all of us every day. We ask questions (Why does my coffee cool so quickly?), we experiment (I'll try this mug today.), and draw conclusions (This cup keeps my coffee warmer.). Yet the thought of teaching a formal experimental process seems confusing, threatening, and even overwhelming. *Building Science Skills* offers easy-to-follow experiments that are fun and motivating for you and your students.

Begin your study of the scientific method with the Whole Class Experiments. These are teacher-led and help familiarize students with the scientific method. Reproducible lab sheets for each experiment guide you and the students through the formal process. Students act as observers, data collectors, and sometimes subjects for these investigations.

For the Individual or Small Group Experiments in the second section, students become the scientists—making observations, recording data, and interpreting results by conducting real experiments themselves. The Assessment Rubric on page 70 may help guide students by graphically showing the expectations.

Beginning on page 72 are guidelines and handouts that help you set up a successful science fair. When your students have learned and practiced the scientific method, this is a great way to showcase their new skills and discoveries.

What Exactly Is the Scientific Method?

Quite often we hear about the results of research or a study. The report often starts out with phrases like "Studies have found" or "Current research says." The scientists doing the research or study used some form of the scientific method to make the discoveries. The scientific method is simply a process that is used to conduct experiments in an organized manner. It is a plan that leads to discovery. It may be formal or informal.

The process begins with a question that needs an answer. Formal and informal experimentation is used, and results are determined. Remember that casual observations are not convincing evidence in the scientific world. Next, true experiments use some means of numeric data collection that is an important component of the scientific method process. Concrete results of an organized experiment are used to make a convincing conclusion. Formal use of the scientific method would control the outside variables that may affect the outcome of an experiment. Results can be easily analyzed and conclusions assumed unbiased if there has been regulation.

Scientific Method Terminology

Conclusion

A conclusion is a logical answer to the original question based on the data and results of the experiment. It tells what is discovered.

Control Group

In an experiment there are usually two or more samples being tested. In order to know if the samples are being affected in the experiment, they have to be compared to something. That something is a sample called the control or control group. The control group is a sample that is treated like the other samples but is not given the experimental variable. For example, in an experiment testing the effect of fertilizer on plant growth, one plant sample receives a large amount of fertilizer, one sample receives a small amount, and one sample receives no fertilizer. The "no fertilizer" sample is the control group. The plants being tested might grow very well without fertilizer. The control group tells you if the experimental variable (fertilizer) has an effect at all. Comparisons to the control group tell you how much of an effect the experimental variable has.

Controlling Variables

In an experiment, it is necessary to control the factors that might affect the experiment. For example, when testing the effect of fertilizer on plants, the variables that are kept exactly the same are water amount and type, soil type, plant type, location, temperature, and container used. All these things could affect the way the plants grow. These are the variables that need to be the same for each plant sample. The only difference between plant samples should be the fertilizer.

Data

Data is the information gathered and recorded during the experiment, including observations and measurements. This information is carefully written down and then organized in chart or graph form.

Discussion

After the experiment is completed, the discussion addresses what was learned, why things may have happened the way they did, what other experiments could be performed, and what changes could be made to make this experiment better.

Experiment

An experiment is the action taken to discover something. It involves testing and trying something with the purpose of learning new information or demonstrating a concept.

Observations

Observations are changes and physical traits noticed by the experimenter by using one or all of the five senses.

Procedure

A procedure is like a recipe. It tells step-by-step how to do the experiment and how to control the variables. Someone else should be able to repeat the experiment when following the procedure.

Question

The question in an experiment is the problem or unknown to which the experimenter is seeking an answer.

Results

Results are what was observed happening during the experiment. These do not tell why events happened, only what happened. They describe changes observed and patterns noticed.

Scientific Method

This is a process that is used to conduct experiments in an organized manner. It may be formal or informal. Formal experiments are written up in an organized manner.

Variables

Anything that can affect the results of an experiment.

Whole Class Experiments

Before students are ready to tackle scientific investigations without teacher guidance, they must have a thorough understanding of the scientific method. To accomplish this task, *Building Science Skills* offers teacher-led Whole Class Experiments.

Each experiment consists of the Teacher Lab Sheet and the Student Lab Sheet. Read the Teacher Lab Sheet in advance, gather materials, and be familiar with the procedure before involving the students. The Teacher Lab Sheet clearly describes how to conduct the experiment. Follow the step-by-step instructions. The Student Lab Sheet is a reproducible worksheet that enables you to guide your students through the experimental process. These are not distributed to the students until the individual experiments have taken place. There is a model of the Student Lab Sheet on page 7. Review this model with your students before you begin this process. Have students attach this model to a folder for easy reference and for a convenient place to keep completed lab sheets.

Complete the experiments in this section in the order given. In the early experiments, students are the subjects. This enhances their interest and motivation. The Teacher Lab Sheet includes examples of possible data, results, conclusions, and discussions. The examples are simply a guide. Student Lab Sheets are partially completed to help students learn the process. The later experiments continue to be led by the teacher, using the instructions found on the Teacher Lab Sheet. The examples of possible data, results, conclusions, and discussions are now eliminated. At this point, the Student Lab Sheets require the students to complete more information, but occasionally offer guiding questions. Students' answers will vary. Look for logical conclusions and discussions that make sense based on the particular results of the experiment. As their skills develop, students will soon be ready to conduct experiments in small groups or individually.

There is no specific time frame for conducting experiments, but it is highly recommended that experiments be done regularly. Regular reinforcement of skills will increase knowledge, comfort level, and confidence in your students. Provide additional modeling by putting each experiment in display form. (See the guidelines under Culminating Event—Science Fair, page 73, to learn how.) Students will become familiar with the process and the expectations of a science fair display.

Some experiments are enhanced when students do some preliminary research. This background knowledge is valuable in drawing conclusions, writing a discussion, and ultimately in designing new experiments. Experiment results may also motivate students to investigate a topic further. Encourage students to continue their investigations. This inquiry leads to further discovery.

Student lab sheet

Name: _____ Date: _____

Model Student Lab Sheet

Refer to this model sheet whenever filling out a lab sheet. It will guide you as you record your information.

(?) Question	What is this experiment about? What are you trying to discover? The question you write in this section must be specific, focusing on the exact concept of the experiment.
(⚬) Materials	List the items you use for the experiment, including the product names. Be specific in the amounts needed and used, as this may have an affect on the final outcome of the experiment.
(⟲) Procedure	The procedure is like a recipe. It tells step-by-step how to do the experiment. Someone completely unfamiliar with the subject should be able to read and follow the procedure and be successful with the experiment. Remember that in an experiment everything should be kept the same each time it is performed. This is called "controlling the variable."
(≣) Data	The data is the numeric result of your experiment. This is often shown in a graph or chart to make the information clearer for the people seeing the results.
(🔍) Result	This section includes a detailed description of what you saw happening during the experiment. You will not tell why something happened, only what happened. Changes and patterns that take place during the experiment are also mentioned, since these may have an effect on the outcome.
(📋) Conclusion	What was discovered? This is the answer to the original question. The answer must be based on the results of the experiment, not on opinions.
(💬) Discussion	In this section, you talk about the experiment. Include what you knew about the subject and the new information you learned. Tell about why you believe things happened the way they did, what you believe went wrong or especially right, and the effects of those events on the experiment. Discuss what you might do differently next time and other experiments that could be done to answer a similar question. Write down ideas on how to make the experiment better.

© McGraw-Hill Children's Publishing   **7**   IF19216 *Building Science Skills*

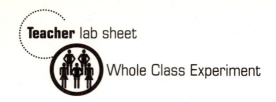

Whole Class Experiment

What's in a Name?

 **Question**

How does advertising affect soda preference in students?

 Materials

- two 2-liter bottles of store-brand soda
- one empty 2-liter bottle of name-brand soda
- small paper cups (two per student)
- paper and pencil

Procedure

Without student knowledge, fill the empty name-brand soda bottle with store-brand soda. Students will be sampling the same brand of soda but will believe they are sampling two different brands. Tell students they will be taking a soda taste test. Their task is to choose the soda they like best. Give each student two empty cups. Pour a sample of each soda into the cups. Be sure the student knows which sample is supposed to be the name-brand soda and which is the store-brand soda. Instruct the students to taste each sample and, without verbal comment, write down their favorite. Collect the ballots. Clean up.

After the experiment is completed, pass out the student lab sheets, revealing the true purpose of this experiment. As a class, review the question, materials, and procedure. Tally the votes and record the data. Brainstorm ways to pictorially show data (chart, bar graph, pie chart). Continue as a group to complete the result, conclusion, and discussion sections.

 Data

Example of Possible Data:
- 19 students liked name brand soda best
- 2 students liked store-brand soda best
- 2 students liked neither sample

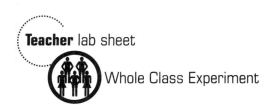

What's in a Name?
(Continued)

 Result

Example of Results:
Both samples given were the same kind of soda, store brand. Students thought they were sampling a name-brand soda and a store-brand soda. Nineteen students liked the name-brand soda best, two students liked the store brand best, and two students did not like either soda drink. Some students wrote down a preference before tasting, some made comments out loud.

 Conclusion

Example of Conclusion:
Of the 23 students participating in this experiment, 19 liked the soda from the name-brand container best even though it contained the store-brand soda. Advertising has made this soda well-known and popular. This experiment has shown that students will choose the famous, popular drink more often than a less popular brand.

 Discussion

Example of Discussion:
This name-brand soda has many commercials and advertisements that appeal to young people. Some students choose it before even tasting it, which shows that something other than taste has influenced them. Other experiments could involve showing commercials for a different name-brand soda first, then holding the taste test. Giving the samples to each student privately might eliminate peer pressure. Testing more students or different age groups may change the results.

Student lab sheet

Whole Class Experiment

Name: _____ Date: _____

What's in a Name?
(Page 1 of 2)

❓ Question

How does advertising affect soda preference in students?

🧪 Materials

- two 2-liter bottles of store-brand soda
- one empty 2-liter bottle of name-brand soda
- small paper cups (two per student)
- paper and pencil

🔄 Procedure

Without student knowledge, fill the empty name-brand soda bottle with store-brand soda. Students will be sampling the same brand of soda but will believe they are tasting two different brands. Tell students they will be taking a soda taste test. Their task is to choose the soda they like best. Give each student two empty cups. Pour a sample of each soda into the cups. Be sure the student knows which sample is the name-brand soda and which is the store-brand soda. Instruct the students to taste each sample and, without verbal comment, write down their favorite. Collect the ballots. Clean up. Tally results.

(In this experiment, everyone was given the same sample at the same time, using the same cups. The only thing different was the type of soda bottle. The control is the store-brand soda, that is what the name brand is being compared to and that is the sample least affected by advertising.)

📊 Data

Data for What's in a Name?

	Name Brand	Store Brand	Other
Number of Students:			

© McGraw-Hill Children's Publishing   IF19216 Building Science Skills

Student lab sheet

Whole Class Experiment

Name: _____ Date: _____

What's in a Name?
(Page 2 of 2)

Result

_____
_____
_____
_____
_____
_____

Conclusion

_____
_____
_____
_____
_____
_____

Discussion

_____
_____
_____
_____
_____
_____

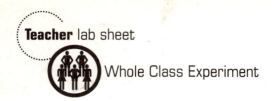

Teacher lab sheet
Whole Class Experiment

Popcorn Party

 Question

Do students prefer the leading brand of popcorn?

 Materials

- leading brand of microwave popcorn
- store brand microwave popcorn
- other brand microwave popcorn
- small paper cups, three per student
- microwave
- three bowls labeled A, B, and C
- paper for ballots and pencil

 Procedure

In advance, microwave each brand of popcorn in the same oven for the same length of time. Without the students' knowledge, pour the leading brand popcorn into bowl A, the store brand into bowl B, and the other brand into bowl C. Keep the brand name of the popcorn a secret. Refer to the brands only by letter. Set the bowls on a table in front of the classroom.

Give students three cups each. Have them label the cups A, B, and C with a pen or pencil. Pass out the ballots. Explain to the students that each person will sample three brands of popcorn and vote for the one he or she likes best.

Call students up to take a cup full of each brand of popcorn, making sure that they label their cups correctly. Students return to their seats to begin tasting the popcorn. After sampling each brand of popcorn, the students vote on their favorite. Collect the ballots. Finish eating any leftover popcorn. Clean up.

After the experiment is completed, pass out the Student Lab Sheets. Review the question, materials, and procedure sections. Count the ballots so students can record the data. Reveal the name brand of each sample of popcorn. Make a graph or chart showing the results. Continue as a group to complete the result, conclusion, and discussion sections.

© McGraw-Hill Children's Publishing   IF19216 *Building Science Skills*

Teacher lab sheet

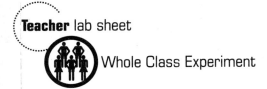 Whole Class Experiment

Popcorn Party
(Continued)

 Data

Example of Data:

Data for Popcorn Party

A Brand 1	B Brand 2	C Brand 3
Number of Students: 6	7	11

 Result

Example of Results:
Students sampled three kinds of popcorn without knowing the brand name. Sample A was XX brand, sample B was YY brand, and sample C was ZZ brand. Six students preferred brand A, 7 students preferred brand B, and 11 preferred brand C. Two students did not like the popcorn but made a choice anyway. All students tasted each sample carefully and made a serious decision.

 Conclusion

Example of Conclusion:
In this experiment, students did not prefer the leading brand of popcorn. Of the 24 students participating in this experiment, almost twice as many students (11) preferred the non-leading brand of popcorn compared to the 6 students who preferred the leading brand. When they did not know the name of the brand being sampled, most students took their time tasting and making a decision based on preference.

 Discussion

Example of Discussion:
Companies spend millions of dollars advertising their products, trying to convince us that they are the best. This experiment shows that what we know about a product from advertising is not always true. In a future experiment, a rating scale could be used to discover which aspect of the popcorn students like best.

Student lab sheet

Whole Class Experiment

Name: _____ Date: _____

Popcorn Party
(Page 1 of 2)

❓ Question

Do students prefer the leading brand of popcorn?

🧾 Materials

- leading brand of microwave popcorn
- store brand microwave popcorn
- other brand microwave popcorn
- small paper cups, three per student
- microwave
- three bowls labeled A, B, and C
- paper for ballots and pencil

🔄 Procedure

In advance, microwave each brand of popcorn in the same oven for the same length of time. Without the students' knowledge, pour the leading brand popcorn into bowl A, the store brand into bowl B, and the other brand into bowl C. Keep the brand name of the popcorn a secret. Refer to the brands only by letter. Set the bowls on a table in front of the classroom.

Give students three cups each. Have them label the cups A, B, and C with a pen or pencil. Pass out the ballots. Explain to the students that each person will sample three brands of popcorn and vote for the one they like best.

Call students up to take a cup full of each brand of popcorn, making sure that they fill the cups correctly. Students return to their seats to begin tasting the popcorn. After sampling each brand of popcorn, the students vote on their favorite. Collect the ballots. Finish eating any leftover popcorn. Clean up.

(In this experiment, everyone was given the same popcorn samples, made in the same manner for the same length of time. The only thing different was the brand of popcorn used. The control group is the store brand popcorn because that is not a nationally advertised brand and the other brands are being compared to it.)

© McGraw-Hill Children's Publishing   IF19216 Building Science Skills

Student lab sheet

Whole Class Experiment

Name: _____ Date: _____

Popcorn Party
(Page 2 of 2)

Data

Data for Popcorn Party

_____ Brand 1	_____ Brand 2	_____ Brand 3
Number of Students:		

Result

_____

_____

_____

_____

Conclusion

_____

_____

_____

_____

Discussion

_____

_____

_____

_____

Teacher lab sheet

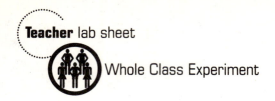 Whole Class Experiment

Math Test—Hard or Easy?

❓ Question

How does perceived test difficulty affect math test results?

📎 Materials

- copies of the math tests (pages 20, 21, and 22)
- pencil
- clock/timer

🔲 Procedure

The problems on the math tests found on pages 20, 21, and 22 are identical. The only differences are the order of the problems and the labels of "Hard" and "Easy." Tell students that approximately one third of the class will take the test labeled "Hard," one third will take the test labeled "Easy," and the remainder of the students will take the test that is not labeled. They have five minutes to work on the test and should not talk.

Shuffle the test papers and randomly hand them out facedown to students. Note the time and then instruct the students to turn over their papers and begin the test. Announce the end of the test after five minutes. Collect the test papers.

Correct the papers using either total number correct or a percentage correct. Group the tests according to labeled difficulty level. Chart the results.

After the experiment is completed, pass out the Student Lab Sheets. Share the raw data with the students, then have individuals or small groups calculate the average score for each testing level. As a group, complete the Student Lab Sheet.

📊 Data

Example of Data for Math Test – Hard or Easy?

	Easy Test Scores	Hard Test Scores	No Label Test Scores
	25	25	25
	23	25	25
	20	24	23
	17	22	20
	15	20	18
	14	17	17
	12	16	17
	12	15	16
Total Score:	138	164	161
Average Score:	17	21	20

© McGraw-Hill Children's Publishing 16 IF19216 Building Science Skills

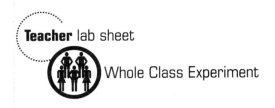

Math Test—Hard or Easy?
(Continued)

Example of Results:
A multiplication math test was given to 24 fifth grade students. Students took a test labeled either "Hard," "Easy," or not labeled, though the problems on each test were identical. Students who took the "Hard" test answered an average of 21 correct out of 25. Those who took the "Easy" test averaged a score of 17 out of 25, and those who took the non-labeled test averaged 20 correct out of 25. The majority completed the test in the five minutes given. None of the students knew that all tests contained the same problems. Some comments were made about how "easy" or "difficult" the test was.

Example of Conclusion:
This experiment has shown that on average students performed better on a math test they perceived as being hard compared to those students who took the same test that was not labeled hard or easy. Students who took the same math test but believed it to be easy got fewer correct answers than those that took the same test labeled hard and those that took the same test with no label. Students performed the best on the test they believed to be more difficult than the others.

Example of Discussion:
We often assume that if something is easy we will do a better job at it than if something is hard. In this experiment, students got more correct answers on a math test they believed to be harder than an "easy" test or the same test with no label. They did a better job on the harder task. This could be because the desire to do well was motivating. Students may have concentrated harder and had better focus. Students taking the "easy" test may not have felt the need to try as hard and made careless errors.

Another experiment could have each student take three tests of equal difficulty but labeled differently. This way all students of varying math ability would be taking each test.

© McGraw-Hill Children's Publishing   17   IF19216 *Building Science Skills*

Student lab sheet

Whole Class Experiment

Name: _____ Date: _____

Math Test—Hard or Easy?
(Page 1 of 2)

? Question

How does perceived test difficulty affect math test results?

Materials

• copies of the math tests (pages 20, 21, and 22)
• pencil
• clock/timer

Procedure

The problems on the math tests found on pages 20, 21, and 22 are identical. The only differences are the order of the problems and the label of "Hard" and "Easy." Tell students that approximately one third of the class will take the test labeled "Hard," one third will take the test labeled "Easy," and the remainder of the students will take the test that is not labeled. They have five minutes to work on the test and should not talk.

Shuffle the test papers and randomly hand them out facedown to students. Note the time and then instruct the students to turn over their papers and begin the test. Announce the end of the test after five minutes. Collect the test papers.

Correct the papers using either total number correct or a percentage correct. Group the tests according to labeled difficulty level. Chart the results.

(In this experiment, everyone was given the same math test at the same time for the same length of time. The only difference was the label on the test paper. The control group is those students taking the test with no label. Tests are not usually labeled hard or easy, and those taking this test are not affected by this kind of label.)

Data

On a separate sheet of paper, calculate the total score and average score for each type of test. Enter the scores on the chart on page 19.

Student lab sheet

Whole Class Experiment

Name: _____ Date: _____

Math Test—Hard or Easy?
(Page 2 of 2)

Data for
Math Test—Hard or Easy?

	Easy Test Scores	Hard Test Scores	No Label Test Scores
Total Score:			
Average Score:			

Result

_____

_____

Conclusion

_____

_____

Discussion

_____

_____

© McGraw-Hill Children's Publishing   **19**   IF19216 *Building Science Skills*

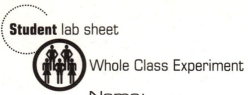

Name: _____ Date: _____

Math Test—Hard

1. 16
   x 2

2. 27
   x 3

3. 10
   x 10

4. 15
   x 3

5.   1
   x 6

6. 63
   x 9

7. 54
   x 10

8.   8
   x 7

9. 39
   x 4

10. 23
   x 16

11. 41
   x 12

12. 72
   x 35

13. 97
   x 8

14. 48
   x 48

15. 12
   x 12

16. 8
   x 6

17. 7
   x 4

18. 19
   x 9

19. 6
   x 3

20. 7
   x 6

21. 36
   x 17

22. 50
   x 31

23. 49
   x 29

24. 70
   x 48

25. 92
   x 8

Student lab sheet

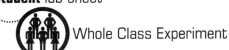
Whole Class Experiment

Name: _____ Date: _____

Math Test—Easy

1. 92
   x 8

2. 70
   x 48

3. 49
   x 29

4. 50
   x 31

5. 36
   x 17

6.   7
   x 6

7.   6
   x 3

8. 19
   x 9

9.   7
   x 4

10. 8
    x 6

11. 12
    x 12

12. 48
    x 48

13. 97
    x 8

14. 72
    x 35

15. 41
    x 12

16. 23
    x 16

17. 39
    x 4

18.   8
    x 7

19. 54
    x 10

20. 63
    x 9

21.   1
    x 6

22. 15
    x 3

23. 10
    x 10

24. 27
    x 3

25. 16
    x 2

McGraw-Hill Children's Publishing   IF19216 *Building Science Skills*

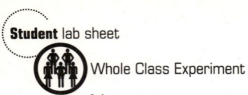

Name: _____ Date: _____

Math Test

1. 49
    x 29

2. 19
    x 9

3. 97
    x 8

4.   8
    x 7

5. 10
    x 10

6. 27
    x 3

7. 54
    x 10

8. 72
    x 35

9.   7
    x 4

10. 50
    x 31

11. 36
    x 17

12. 8
    x 6

13. 41
    x 12

14. 63
    x 9

15. 16
    x 2

16. 1
    x 6

17. 23
    x 16

18. 12
    x 12

19. 7
    x 6

20. 92
    x 8

21. 70
    x 48

22. 6
    x 3

23. 48
    x 48

24. 39
    x 4

25. 15
    x 3

Teacher lab sheet

Whole Class Experiment

Silence Is Golden

 Question

Does the style of background music affect math test results?

 Materials

- copies of math tests (pages 28, 29, and 30)
- audiotape or CD player
- recorded vocal music
- recorded instrumental music
- pencil
- clock/timer

Procedure

The math tests found on pages 28, 29, and 30 contain different problems but are equal in difficulty. Give one test with no background music. Students should not talk. Time the test for five minutes. Collect the tests. Give the second test while playing a vocal music selection, again for five minutes. Collect the tests. Give the third test for five minutes while playing the instrumental music selection. Collect the tests.

Correct the papers, indicating either a percentage grade or number of correct answers. Share the data with the students. Have them calculate a class average score for each test. Complete the Student Lab Sheet as a group, including the materials and procedure. If students are comfortable, they may work in small groups to complete the Student Lab Sheets and make a graph of the data. Then review the Lab Sheet as a whole group.

When complete, return individual math tests. Students can look at how background music affects their individual test results. Have students discuss how individual results compare to class averages and how they feel about having background music.

© McGraw-Hill Children's Publishing — IF19216 *Building Science Skills*

Student lab sheet

Whole Class Experiment

Name: _____ Date: _____

Silence Is Golden
(Page 1 of 4)

(?) Question

Does the style of background music affect math test results?

(§) Materials

_____

_____

_____

_____

(⊟) Procedure

What is done first?

_____

_____

What is done next?

_____

_____

What is done last?

_____

_____

(In this experiment, everyone was given the same math tests, at the same time, for the same length of time. The only difference was the type of background music. The control group is those students taking the test with no background music. This is the way tests are usually given. The scores from the other tests are compared to this test.)

© McGraw-Hill Children's Publishing   **24**   IF19216 *Building Science Skills*

Student lab sheet

Whole Class Experiment

Name: _____ Date: _____

Silence Is Golden
(Page 2 of 4)

Data

Complete the chart shown below. Record the number of problems answered correctly by each student for each test.

Student Name	No Music	Vocal Music	Instrumental Music
Silence Is Golden Data			
Student #1			
Student #2			
Student #3			
Student #4			
Student #5			
Student #6			
Student #7			
Student #8			
Student #9			
Student #10			
Student #11			
Student #12			
Student #13			
Student #14			
Student #15			
Student #16			
Student #17			
Student #18			
Student #19			
Student #20			
Student #21			
Student #22			
Student #23			
Student #24			
Student #25			
Student #26			
Student #27			
Student #28			
Student #29			
Student #30			
Total Score:			
Average Score:			

© McGraw-Hill Children's Publishing

IF19216 *Building Science Skills*

Student lab sheet

Whole Class Experiment

Name: _____ Date: _____

Silence Is Golden
(Page 3 of 4)

Result

In sentence form, tell what the average scores are for each music type.

_____
_____
_____
_____
_____

Conclusion

Look at the data. Does background music type affect test scores?

_____
_____
_____
_____
_____

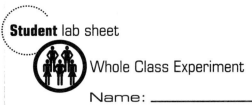

Student lab sheet

Whole Class Experiment

Name: _____ Date: _____

Silence Is Golden
(Page 4 of 4)

 **Discussion**

How are tests usually given in school? Is there a lot of noise or music? What did you learn about the affect of background music on test scores from this experiment?

_____
_____
_____

Did anything go wrong? What could be done differently to make this experiment better?

_____
_____
_____

Did this experiment make you think of any other questions? Are there other experiments, similar to this one, that you would like to try?

_____
_____
_____
_____
_____
_____

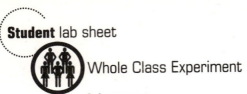

Name: _____ Date: _____

Silence Is Golden
Math Test I

1. 15
   x 2

2.   6
   x 8

3.   0
   x 0

4. 24
   x 4

5. 16
   x 8

6.   9
   x 4

7. 80
   x 5

8.   8
   x 3

9. 41
   x 5

10. 18
   x 11

11. 47
   x 6

12. 28
   x 16

13. 62
   x 7

14. 39
   x 29

15. 7
   x 1

16. 54
   x 46

17. 93
   x 4

18. 8
   x 7

19. 61
   x 30

20. 74
   x 3

21. 6
   x 3

22. 76
   x 14

23. 35
   x 5

24. 9
   x 5

25. 80
   x 40

© McGraw-Hill Children's Publishing   IF19216 Building Science Skills

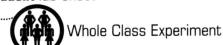

Name: _____ Date: _____

Silence Is Golden
Math Test II

1.
   6
x 6

2.
  86
x 7

3.
  24
x 16

4.
  5
x 3

5.
  39
x 2

6.
  91
x 5

7.
  41
x 21

8.
  7
x 6

9.
  51
x 6

10.
  63
x 60

11.
  75
x 0

12.
  9
x 0

13.
  68
x 4

14.
  27
x 10

15.
  4
x 4

16.
  12
x 9

17.
  32
x 29

18.
  3
x 3

19.
  42
x 8

20.
  80
x 7

21.
  8
x 5

22.
  58
x 42

23.
  17
x 6

24.
  2
x 1

25.
  97
x 91

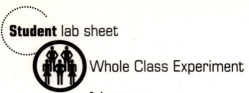

Name: _____ **Date:** _____

Silence Is Golden
Math Test III

1.
   1
x 0

2.
  31
x 1

3.
  64
x 11

4.
  6
x 3

5.
  76
x 9

6.
  47
x 8

7.
  8
x 3

8.
  16
x 12

9.
  65
x 5

10.
  70
x 46

11.
  7
x 6

12.
  40
x 7

13.
  52
x 6

14.
  21
x 18

15.
  3
x 2

16.
  4
x 1

17.
  26
x 2

18.
  38
x 27

19.
  9
x 4

20.
  99
x 4

21.
  88
x 3

22.
  81
x 77

23.
  5
x 5

24.
  49
x 48

25.
  10
x 5

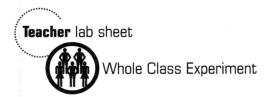

Teacher lab sheet

Whole Class Experiment

Iced Batteries

 Question

How does temperature affect battery life?

 Materials

- flashlight
- identical flashlight batteries
- clock/timer
- thermometer
- refrigerator/freezer

 Procedure

One month before performing this experiment, place two batteries in a refrigerator and two batteries in a freezer. Record the date and temperature of each location. Store the remaining batteries at room temperature in a closet or drawer until ready to perform the experiment.

Begin with the room temperature batteries. Place them inside the flashlight. Turn the flashlight on and record the time to the nearest second. Set the flashlight down where it can be observed without being touched. Time how long the flashlight shines, until no more glow is seen in the bulb. Calculate the length of time the battery lasted (subtract the beginning time from the ending time). Should the light continue to shine at the end of the school day, shut the flashlight off, record the time, and continue the next morning, adding together the length of time the light shone each day.

Repeat the procedure using the batteries from the refrigerator. Record the length of time the flashlight shone with these batteries. Repeat again with the batteries from the freezer.

After the experiment is completed, pass out Student Lab Sheets. Post the data. Have students work in small groups to complete the Lab Sheets and to make a chart or graph of the data. Review as a whole group.

© McGraw-Hill Children's Publishing   **31**   IF19216 *Building Science Skills*

Student lab sheet

Whole Class Experiment

Name: _____ Date: _____

Iced Batteries
(Page 1 of 3)

? Question

How does temperature affect battery life?

Materials

_____
_____
_____
_____
_____

Procedure

What is done first?
_____
_____

What is done next?
_____
_____

What is done last?
_____
_____

(Note that the only variable that was different was the temperature at which the batteries were stored. These batteries are the control group.)

Student lab sheet

Whole Class Experiment

Name: _____ Date: _____

Iced Batteries
(Page 2 of 3)

Data

Record the data on the chart below.

Data for Iced Batteries

	Battery at Room Temp.	Battery at ____ degrees	Battery at ____ degrees
Length of Battery Life (hr. and min.)			

Result

In sentence form, tell the length of time each battery lasted at each temperature.

_____

_____

_____

What did you observe during the experiment? Were there any patterns? Did anything unusual happen? Write down any observations you feel are important.

_____

_____

_____

_____

© McGraw-Hill Children's Publishing   IF19216 *Building Science Skills*

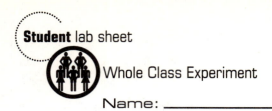

Iced Batteries
(Page 3 of 3)

Conclusion

Look at the data. Does temperature affect battery life?

_____
_____
_____
_____

Discussion

Some people believe storing batteries in the refrigerator will help them last longer. Does it?

_____
_____

What did you learn about the affect of temperature on batteries from this experiment?

_____
_____
_____

Did anything go wrong? What could be done differently to make this experiment better?

_____
_____

Did this experiment make you think of any other questions? Are there other experiments, similar to this one, that you would like to try?

_____
_____
_____

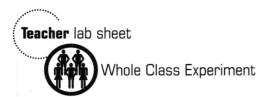

Teacher lab sheet

Whole Class Experiment

Let It Grow! Let It Grow!

 Question

How does light affect grass growth?

 Materials

- 45 mL (3 Tbsp.) grass seed, along with the seed package
- 711 mL (approximately 3 cups) potting soil
- 3 small paper cups
- water
- ruler
- tablespoon

 Procedure

Label the paper cups as follows: windowsill, shelf, and closet. Pour potting soil into each cup about 25 mm (1 inch) from the top. Sprinkle 15 mL (1 Tbsp.) of grass seed into each cup. Sprinkle 15 mL (1 Tbsp.) of water over the seeds. Give each cup of grass seed 15 mL (1 Tbsp.) of water each day. The amount of water may be adjusted as the grass grows, but give each cup the same amount.

Place the cup labeled "windowsill" on a windowsill (sunny location if possible). Place the cup labeled "shelf" on a shelf away from the windows. Place the cup labeled "closet" in a dark closet.

Each day record the date and length (in centimeters) of the tallest grass blade from each cup. Allow two weeks for this experiment from the time the first seeds sprout.

Pass out Student Lab Sheets. Have students work in small groups to create graphs of the results and to complete the Lab Sheets. An option would be to give the students the Lab Sheets at the beginning of the experiment so they can record the data each day for the duration of the experiment.

© McGraw-Hill Children's Publishing

IF19216 Building Science Skills

Student lab sheet

Whole Class Experiment

Name: _____ Date: _____

Let It Grow! Let It Grow!
(Page 1 of 4)

? Question

How does light affect grass growth?

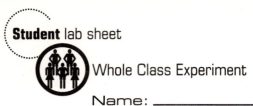

Materials

_____
_____

Procedure

What is done first?
_____
_____

What is done next?
_____
_____

What is done last?
_____
_____

(In this experiment, the same type of grass seed was grown in the same type of cups, with the same soil, and the same amount of water. The only difference between each group was the amount of light the plants received. The control group was the cup placed on the windowsill, because that is the natural type of light grass would get.)

© McGraw-Hill Children's Publishing   IF19216 *Building Science Skills*

Student lab sheet

Whole Class Experiment

Name: _____ Date: _____

Let It Grow! Let It Grow!
(Page 2 of 4)

Data

Record the height, in centimeters, of the tallest blade of grass in each sample and the date.

Data for Let It Grow! Let It Grow!

Date	Windowsill Sample	Shelf Sample	Closet Sample
	0 cm	0 cm	0 cm

© McGraw-Hill Children's Publishing   IF19216 *Building Science Skills*

Student lab sheet

Whole Class Experiment

Name: _____ Date: _____

Let It Grow! Let It Grow!
(Page 3 of 4)

🔍 Result

In sentence form, describe the overall growth of each grass sample. For example, "At the end of two weeks the grass plants on the windowsill grew 15 centimeters."

_____
_____
_____

What did you observe during the experiment? Were there any patterns? Did anything unusual happen? Write down any observations you feel are important.

_____
_____
_____

📋 Conclusion

Look at the data. Does light affect grass growth? Explain.

_____
_____
_____

Student lab sheet

Whole Class Experiment

Name: _____ Date: _____

Let It Grow! Let It Grow!
(Page 4 of 4)

💬 Discussion

Grass grows in a variety of locations, some sunny all the time, some shady. Look at the grass seed package. What type of location is best for these seeds? How well did they grow in the locations of this experiment?

_____

_____

_____

What did you learn about light and grass growth from this experiment?

_____

_____

_____

Did anything go wrong? What could be done differently to make this experiment better?

_____

_____

_____

Did this experiment make you think of any other questions? Are there other experiments, similar to this one, that you would like to try?

_____

_____

_____

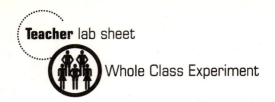

How Long Will It Go?

Does a name-brand alkaline battery really last longer?

• three identical flashlights
• batteries for the flashlights: a name-brand alkaline battery, another alkaline brand, and a non-alkaline battery
• timer/clock

Place batteries in the flashlights. Label each flashlight with the name of the battery inside it. Request the assistance of three volunteers. Have them turn on the flashlights at the same time. Record the time to the nearest second. Set the flashlights on a flat surface where the lights can be observed. If no one is available to observe the lights, turn off the flashlights simultaneously and record the time. Continue the experiment when lights can again be observed, being certain to record the start and end times.

Record the time when each light goes out. Have students calculate the length of time each light lasted (subtract the beginning time from the ending time).

Pass out the Student Lab Sheets. Have students complete the sheets individually or in small groups. Review as a whole class.

Student lab sheet

Whole Class Experiment

Name: _____ Date: _____

How Long Will It Go?
(Page 1 of 4)

(?) Question

Does the name-brand battery really last longer?

(§) Materials

_____

_____

(⊡) Procedure

What is done first?

_____

_____

What is done next?

_____

_____

What is done last?

_____

_____

(In this experiment, the same type of flashlights are used, they are on at the same time, and in the same place. Only the batteries are different. The control group is the non-alkaline battery.)

Student lab sheet

Whole Class Experiment

Name: _____ Date: _____

How Long Will It Go?

(Page 2 of 4)

Data

Record the length of time each battery kept the flashlight lit in the chart shown below.

Data for How Long Will It Go?

	Flashlight with non-alkaline batteries	Flashlight with _____ batteries	Flashlight with _____ batteries
Time			

Result

In sentence form, tell the length of time each battery lasted, beginning with the longest.

_____

_____

_____

_____

What did you observe during the experiment? Were there any patterns? Did anything unusual happen? Write down any observations you feel are important.

_____

_____

_____

_____

© McGraw-Hill Children's Publishing   IF19216 *Building Science Skills*

Student lab sheet

Whole Class Experiment

Name: _____ Date: _____

How Long Will It Go?
(Page 3 of 4)

📋 Conclusion

Look at the data. In this experiment, did the name-brand alkaline battery last longer? Explain.

_____
_____
_____
_____
_____

💬 Discussion

Tell what you know about name-brand batteries from commercials and other advertisements. Did the results of this experiment agree with what the commercials say? Explain your answer.

_____
_____
_____
_____
_____
_____
_____

What did you learn about battery life from this experiment?

_____
_____
_____
_____
_____

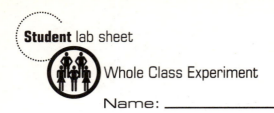

How Long Will It Go?
(Page 4 of 4)

Did anything go wrong? What could be done differently to make this experiment better?

_____
_____
_____
_____
_____
_____

Did this experiment make you think of any other questions? Are there other experiments, similar to this one, that you would like to try?

_____
_____
_____
_____
_____
_____

Individual or Small Group Experiments

The experiments in this section can be completed by students who are working independently or in small groups of two to four members. The directions for each experiment consist of a materials list and a procedure. The standard reproducible lab sheets found on pages 46–48 are for use with all of the following experiments. Remind the students that they should refer to the Student Lab Sheet model found on page 7 if they need guidance with any of the sections and the requirements for them. Read the experiment in advance so preparations and materials can be gathered.

When working in small groups, it is recommended that a formal, cooperative grouping method be used. Assigning roles such as facilitator, measurer, recorder, and reporter will help the group work together as a team and prevent one member from taking over and other members from doing very little. Defining and clarifying the responsibilities of each role is an important step to take. Place cards can be made to help students remember their roles and responsibilities.

The role of facilitator is primarily that of an organizer/coordinator/leader. The responsibilities include making sure everyone knows what to do and that everyone is helping and staying on task. The measurer is responsible for making the measurements required in the experiment. This person reads the thermometer or uses the ruler/yardstick. The recorder writes down the data collected and makes the chart or graph. The reporter does the physical writing of the rest of the lab sheet based on input from the group. Everyone supports each other in their roles, providing input and suggestions.

The following experiments may be conducted in any order. Conducting experiments regularly helps reinforce skills and builds confidence and a high comfort level in using the scientific method. Information about control groups and controlling variables is given in the procedure. This information is not necessary in the Student Lab Sheet, but is given to remind students of proper experimenting techniques. The Assessment Rubric found on page 70 can be used to provide feedback to students on their lab sheet write-ups. Share the rubric before students complete the experiment so they understand expectations.

Student lab sheet

Individual/Small Group Experiment

Name: _____ Date: _____

Title: _____

(Page 1 of 3)

(?) Question

_____

_____

(§) Materials

_____

_____

_____

(⟲) Procedure

What is done first?

_____

_____

_____

What is done next?

_____

_____

_____

What is done last?

_____

_____

_____

© McGraw-Hill Children's Publishing   IF19216 *Building Science Skills*

Student lab sheet

Individual/Small Group Experiment

Name: _____ Date: _____

Title: _____
(Page 2 of 3)

Data

Use this spot for notes. Use a separate sheet of paper for charts and graphs.

Result

_____

_____

_____

_____

_____

_____

© McGraw-Hill Children's Publishing   IF19216 *Building Science Skills*

Student lab sheet

Individual/Small Group Experiment

Name: _____ Date: _____

Title:_____

(Page 3 of 3)

Conclusion

_____

_____

_____

_____

_____

_____

Discussion

_____

_____

_____

_____

_____

_____

Student lab sheet

Individual/Small Group Experiment

Name: _____ Date: _____

Do Sneakers Help You Jump Higher?

? Question

Do sneakers help you jump higher?

Materials

- pair of sneakers
- pair of street shoes or sandals
- long piece of black paper
- meter stick or tape measure
- tape
- piece of chalk

Procedure

Tape the piece of black paper onto the wall so that the bottom of the paper touches your fingertips when you reach your hand up the wall. To jump, first cover one or two fingertips with chalk. Then stand near the wall, bend at the knees, and jump up. At the same time, reach up with your chalked hand and touch the black paper as high up as you can. This will leave a mark that is used to measure the height of your jump. Always try to jump as high as possible and jump the same way each time (controlled variable). Measure the height, in centimeters, from the floor to the chalk mark. Record the results.

All jumps are made by the same person at the same location (controlled variables). The first jump should be done in bare feet (control group). Make sure the floor is clear of any sharp objects. Perform the jump, measure the height, and record the data. The second jump is done in the street shoes or sandals. Perform the jump the same way as the first, measure the height, and record the data. The final jump is done in sneakers. Again, perform the jump the same way as the first, measure the height, and record the data.

When complete, make a chart or graph of the data. Use the Student Lab Sheet on pages 46–48 to write up the experiment.

Data

Do Sneakers Help You Jump Higher?

	Barefoot Jump	Jump with Shoes or Sandals	Jump with Sneakers
Height (cm)			

© McGraw-Hill Children's Publishing — IF19216 *Building Science Skills*

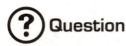

Student lab sheet

Individual/Small Group Experiment

Name: _____ Date: _____

How Does What a Cup Is Made of Affect Insulation?
(Page 1 of 2)

? Question

How does what a cup is made of affect its insulation?

Materials

- measuring cup
- glass jar
- styrene foam cup
- insulated plastic mug
- ceramic mug
- water
- thermometer(s)
- timer/clock

Procedure

Pour hot tap water into the measuring cup. Take the temperature of the water. By adding cold or hot water, adjust the water so that the temperature is 50° C. Pour 120 mL of the water into the jar. Set the jar on a flat surface where it will not be touched, such as a desktop or table. Start the timer. The temperature at zero minutes is 50° C, as shown on the data chart. After five minutes, take the temperature of the water. Record the result. Take another temperature reading after 10 minutes and again after 15 minutes.

Measure another 120 mL of hot water. Take the temperature and adjust it until the thermometer reads 50° C. Pour the water into the ceramic mug. Set the mug in the same area as the jar, though not in the exact same spot. This spot may still be warm from the jar. The temperature at zero minutes is 50° C. After 5 minutes, take a temperature reading and record. Repeat at 10- and 15-minute intervals.

Repeat the procedure for the insulated plastic mug and the styrene foam cup. If more than one thermometer is available, two or more mugs may be tested at the same time. Record all temperature readings. Make a graph of the results and complete the Student Lab Sheet.

The control group is the glass jar because jars are not thought of as having any insulation value. The jar represents a mug with no insulation. The variables being controlled are the starting temperature of the water, the amount of water, the room temperature, and where the mugs are placed.

© McGraw-Hill Children's Publishing   IF19216 *Building Science Skills*

Student lab sheet

Individual/Small Group Experiment

Name: _____ Date: _____

How Does What a Cup Is Made of Affect Insulation?
(Page 2 of 2)

Data

Data for Cup Material Affecting Insulation

		Jar	Ceramic Mug	Plastic Mug	Foam Mug
Water Temperature	At 0 min.				
	At 5 min.				
	At 10 min.				
	At 15 min.				

© McGraw-Hill Children's Publishing   **51**   IF19216 *Building Science Skills*

Student lab sheet

 Individual/Small Group Experiment

Name: _____ Date: _____

How Does Acid Rain Affect Grass Growth?
(Page 1 of 2)

? Question

How does acid rain affect grass growth?

Materials

- 3 styrene foam cups
- potting soil
- 15 mL (1 Tbsp.) grass seed
- a spoon
- 360 mL (12 oz.) jar with lid
- measuring cup or beaker
- water
- vinegar
- metric ruler
- scissors

Procedure

Label the cups A, B, and C. Pour equal amounts of potting soil into each foam cup. Sprinkle 5 mL of grass seed on top of the soil of each cup. Give each cup 15 mL of water. Set the cups together in an appropriate place (windowsill, shelf). Each day, give the seeds 5 mL of water. Continue watering until the grass plants are at least 6 cm tall (this may take two or more weeks).

Meanwhile, prepare a vinegar solution by measuring 240 mL of water and pouring it into the jar. Add to the jar 120 mL of vinegar. Stir gently. Save until ready to use. Vinegar is an acid. This solution represents acid rain.

When grass blades are at least 6 cm tall, the important part of the experiment begins. With scissors, trim the grass in each cup to a height of 5 cm. The data chart shows this initial height. Water cup A with 5 mL of regular water just as you have been. Water cup B with 5 mL of vinegar solution from the jar. Water cup C with 5 mL of undiluted vinegar.

On Day 2, measure the height of the grass and record any other observations. Water each cup as described above: cup A—regular water, cup B—vinegar solution, and cup C—vinegar.

Continue in this manner for 14 days. Complete the Student Lab Sheet.

In this experiment, the control is the grass being watered with regular tap water. Be sure to control variables such as the amount of light, amount of water, and type of soil.

© McGraw-Hill Children's Publishing — IF19216 *Building Science Skills*

Student lab sheet

Individual/Small Group Experiment

Name: _____ Date: _____

How Does Acid Rain Affect Grass Growth?
(Page 2 of 2)

Data

Data for Acid Rain Affecting Grass Growth

		A	**B**	**C**
Height in Centimeters (cm)	Day 1	5 cm	5 cm	5 cm
	Day 2			
	Day 3			
	Day 4			
	Day 5			
	Day 6			
	Day 7			
	Day 8			
	Day 9			
	Day 10			
	Day 11			
	Day 12			
	Day 13			
	Day 14			

© McGraw-Hill Children's Publishing   IF19216 *Building Science Skills*

Student lab sheet

Individual/Small Group Experiment

Name: _____ Date: _____

How Does Physical Exercise Affect Reaction Time?
(Page 1 of 2)

? Question

How does physical exercise affect reaction time?

Materials

- meter stick
- timer/clock
- volunteer to exercise (called "the subject")

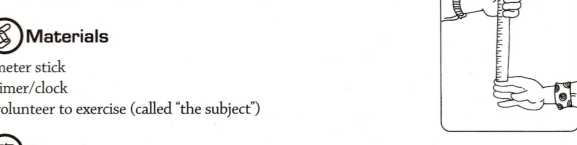

Procedure

Reaction time is measured using a ruler. The subject (exerciser) holds his hand in front of his body ready to grab the ruler. Hold the ruler over the open hand, making sure the zero end is pointing down. Without saying anything, let go of the ruler. Without moving his arm, the subject will try to grab hold of the ruler before it slips through his fingers. Read the number (in centimeters) above the subject's hand. Even though this number usually measures distance, in this experiment it will be used to measure reaction time, the lower the number the faster the reaction time.

Measure the subject's reaction time before physical exercise takes place (control). Record the number. Have the subject do jumping jacks for one minute. At the end of the minute, measure the subject's reaction time and record the data.

Next have the subject do jumping jacks for two minutes. Measure the reaction time and record the data. Finally have the subject do jumping jacks for three minutes, measure reaction time, and record data. Note that the variables are being controlled by using the same exerciser, the exercising takes place in the same place within a short period of time, and reaction time is measured in the same way by the same person.

When the study is complete, make a chart or graph of the data. Use the Student Lab Sheet to write up the experiment.

© McGraw-Hill Children's Publishing   IF19216 *Building Science Skills*

Student lab sheet

Individual/Small Group Experiment

Name: _____ Date: _____

How Does Physical Exercise Affect Reaction Time?
(Page 2 of 2)

Data

	Before Exercise	After 1 minute of Exercise	After 2 minutes of Exercise	After 3 minutes of Exercise
Reaction Time				

If the experiment is repeated with a second subject, record the results below.

	Before Exercise	After 1 minute of Exercise	After 2 minutes of Exercise	After 3 minutes of Exercise
Reaction Time				

© McGraw-Hill Children's Publishing · IF19216 *Building Science Skills*

Student lab sheet

Individual/Small Group Experiment

Name: _____ Date: _____

How Does Weight Affect the Flight of a Paper Airplane?
(Page 1 of 2)

? Question

How does weight affect the flight of a paper airplane?

Materials

- copier paper
- five paper clips (all the same size and kind)
- meter stick
- masking tape

Procedure

Fold a piece of paper to make the paper airplane (see page 57). Find a place to fly the plane. Mark the starting point with a piece of masking tape. Stand with your toes just to the line of masking tape. Throw the plane. You may need to practice flying the plane before actually starting the experiment.

After the plane lands, leave it in that position. Measure how far the plane traveled using the meter stick. Begin at the masking tape mark and measure to the farthest end of the plane. Record the distance in centimeters. This is the control group.

Add a paper clip to the tail end of the plane. Stand at the masking tape starting point and fly the plane again. Throw the plane in the same way and with the same strength used for the first flight. After the plane lands, measure the distance traveled, recording the results.

Add a second paper clip to the tail of the plane. Fly it, measure the distance, and record the results. Continue making trial flights, adding a paper clip each time. The variables are controlled by using the same plane, starting at the same point, and throwing the plane in the same way.

When complete, use the data to make a graph and complete the Student Lab Sheet.

Data

	No Weight	1 Clip	2 Clips	3 Clips	4 Clips	5 Clips
Distance						

© McGraw-Hill Children's Publishing   IF19216 Building Science Skills

Student lab sheet

Individual/Small Group Experiment

Name: _____ Date: _____

How Does Weight Affect the Flight of a Paper Airplane?
(Page 2 of 2)

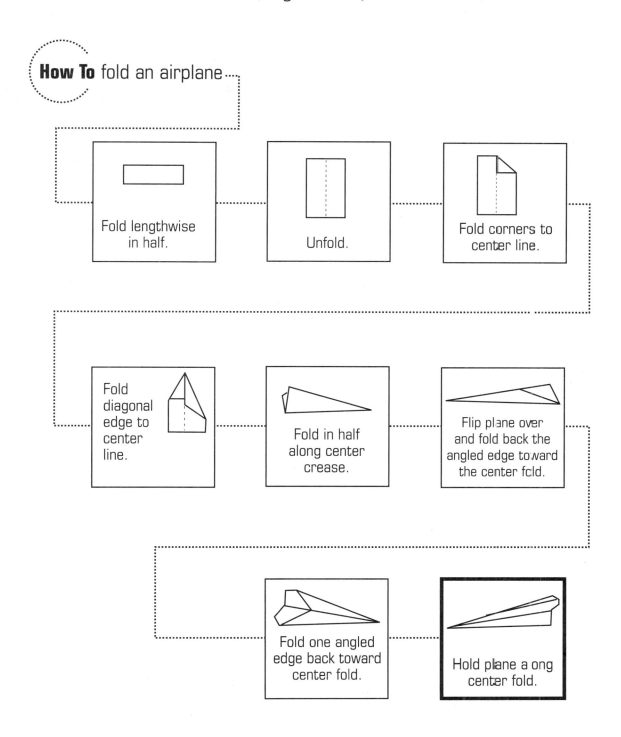

How To fold an airplane

- Fold lengthwise in half.
- Unfold.
- Fold corners to center line.
- Fold diagonal edge to center line.
- Fold in half along center crease.
- Flip plane over and fold back the angled edge toward the center fold.
- Fold one angled edge back toward center fold.
- Hold plane along center fold.

Student lab sheet

Individual/Small Group Experiment

Name: _____ Date: _____

How Does the Color of Food Affect Preference?

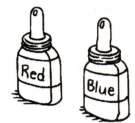

? Question

How does the color of food affect preference?

Materials

- large jar of applesauce
- small paper cups
- plastic spoons
- food coloring
- three identical bowls
- test subjects

Procedure

Pour equal amounts of applesauce into each bowl. Add 3 drops of food coloring to one bowl (any color) and stir thoroughly. Add 3 drops of a different color to the second bowl of applesauce and stir thoroughly. Leave the third bowl of applesauce uncolored. This is the control group because it is the natural color of applesauce.

Now show the subject the three bowls of applesauce. Ask which sauce she would like to sample. Put a tally mark on the data chart under the selection and give the subject the sample of her choice. Repeat for each subject. Ask at least 10 people which applesauce they prefer. The more people asked, the more accurate the results.

Count the tallies for each color applesauce, make a graph, and complete the rest of the Student Lab Sheet.

Data

Applesauce Tallies

	Natural Applesauce	_____ Applesauce	_____ Applesauce
Tallies			
Total			

© McGraw-Hill Children's Publishing

Student lab sheet

Individual/Small Group Experiment

Name: _____ Date: _____

What Color Clothing Keeps You Warmest?

❓ Question

What color clothing keeps you warmest?

🧶 Materials

- white T-shirt
- medium-colored T-shirt (yellow, orange)
- dark-colored T-shirt (navy, black)
- sunny day
- watch/timer
- thermometer

⬚ Procedure

On a sunny day, take your materials outside. Set the thermometer on a table or flat surface. Wait five minutes. Record the temperature (this is the control). Lay the white T-shirt on the same surface as the thermometer, making sure it is spread out flat. Place the thermometer inside the shirt between the two layers of fabric. Wait five minutes. Read and record the temperature. Repeat these steps with the other two T-shirts. The variables are controlled by placing the T-shirts in the same location at about the same time of the day and waiting five minutes for the temperature to adjust.

Make a graph and complete the Student Lab Sheet.

📄 Data

	No Shirt	White T-shirt	Medium-Colored T-shirt	Dark-Colored T-shirt
Temperature				

© McGraw-Hill Children's Publishing   IF19216 Building Science Skills

Student lab sheet

Individual/Small Group Experiment

Name: _____ Date: _____

What Could Be Added to Bubble Solution to Make the Bubbles Last Longer?

(Page 1 of 3)

 **Question**

What could be added to bubble solution to make the bubbles last longer?

 **Materials**

- 75 mL liquid dish detergent
- 300 mL water
- 10 mL table sugar
- 10 mL corn syrup
- another substance to make the bubbles last
- newspapers
- spoon and beaker or measuring cup
- drinking straws
- styrene foam trays
- stopwatch/clock with second hand
- bucket or sink

 **Procedure**

Gather all materials. Cover work area with newspaper. Carefully make the bubble solution in the foam tray by following the formula on page 61. Wet the sides of the tray by dipping your finger in the bubble solution and spreading it around. Dip the end of your straw into the solution then gently blow into the straw to make bubbles in the tray. Don't be surprised if bubbles pop right away. Try to blow bubbles about the same size each time.

To measure how long a bubble lasts, blow a medium-sized bubble (about the size of a tennis ball) and begin timing as soon as you pull the straw away from the bubble. The help of a partner may make timing easier. Your partner can watch the clock while listening to your commands of start and stop.

Blow a medium-sized bubble and time how long the bubble lasts. This first solution is the control group (nothing has been added to make the bubbles last longer). Write down the lasting time in seconds. This is Trial 1. Blow a second bubble, time how long it lasts, and record this time. This is Trial 2. Repeat one more time. This is Trial 3.

Add 5 mL of sugar to the bubble solution in the tray and mix thoroughly. Blow a medium-sized bubble. Time how long this bubble lasts. Record the time under Trial 1 in the data chart. Repeat two more times. Add another 5 mL of sugar to the solution for a total of 10 mL of sugar. Mix gently and thoroughly. Blow a bubble, time how long it lasts, and record the time. Repeat two more times. Carefully dump the solution into a bucket or sink. Briefly rinse the tray to remove any undissolved sugar.

Student lab sheet

Individual/Small Group Experiment

Name: _____ Date: _____

What Could Be Added to Bubble Solution to Make the Bubbles Last Longer?
(Page 2 of 3)

Make another solution in the tray following the formula below. This time add the corn syrup in the same amounts and in the same way as you did the sugar. Carefully record all results. Rinse the tray and begin again.

Make one more bubble solution, this time adding a substance of your choice to the formula, following the directions for adding the sugar. Test this solution, recording the results each time.

Look at your data. Calculate the average time the bubbles lasted for each solution type. Make a graph of the data and complete the Student Lab Sheet.

Bubble Solution Formula

  100 mL water
  25 mL liquid dish detergent

- Pour ingredients into a styrene foam tray.
- Mix gently and thoroughly.

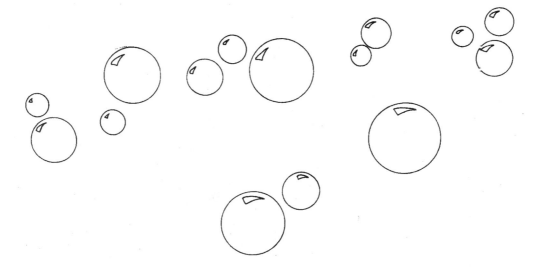

© McGraw-Hill Children's Publishing   IF19216 Building Science Skills

Student lab sheet

Individual/Small Group Experiment

Name: _____ Date: _____

What Could Be Added to Bubble Solution to Make the Bubbles Last Longer?

(Page 3 of 3)

Data

Solution	Trial 1	Trial 2	Trial 3	Average*
Nothing Added				
5 mL Sugar				
10 mL Sugar (total)				
5 mL Corn Syrup				
10 mL Corn Syrup (total)				
1 tsp. _____				
2 tsp. _____				

Length of Time in Seconds

*Solving Averages
To figure out the average, add together the times from Trial 1, Trial 2, and Trial 3. Next divide the total by 3.

For example: 3 sec. + 5 sec. + 4 sec. = 12 sec.
12 sec. ÷ 3 = 4 sec.

Student lab sheet

Individual/Small Group Experiment

Name: _____ Date: _____

How Does Size Affect the Dissolving Rate of Sugar in Water?

(?) Question

How does size affect the dissolving rate of sugar in water?

(§) Materials

- 3 dark-colored hard candies
- 3 clear plastic cups
- 360 mL water
- plastic wrap
- small hammer or rolling pin
- watch/clock with second hand

(⎇) Procedure

Label the plastic cups as samples A, B, and C. Pour 120 mL of water into each cup. Set aside. Wrap one piece of candy in a piece of plastic wrap. Break the candy by crushing it with the rolling pin or gently tapping with a hammer. Continue crushing the candy until it is a fine powder.

You will be timing how long it takes for the candy to dissolve in the cup of water. Pour the powdered candy into the water of sample cup A, begin timing, and observe carefully. Record how long it takes for the candy to completely dissolve.

Wrap the second piece of candy in plastic wrap, break a second piece of candy into five or six large chunks. This is sample B. Sample C is the whole piece of hard candy, which will be placed in the cup labeled C.

Drop both sample B (the large chunks) and sample C (the whole piece of candy) into their cups of water at the same time. Observe the cups and time how long it takes for each sample to dissolve completely. Record the times. Clean up all materials and complete the Student Lab Sheet.

The control group is the powdered piece of candy. Sugar is usually dissolved in liquids in a finer, granulated state. The variables being controlled include the amount of water, the temperature of the water, and the type of sugar used. The only difference is the size of the sugar samples.

(▤) Data

	Sample A (powdered)	Sample B (chunks)	Sample C (whole)
Dissolving Rate			

© McGraw-Hill Children's Publishing   **63**   IF19216 *Building Science Skills*

Student lab sheet

Individual/Small Group Experiment

Name: _____ Date: _____

What Is the Effect of Fertilizer on Grass Growth?
(Page 1 of 2)

❓ Question

What is the effect of fertilizer on grass growth?

🧪 Materials

- 20 mL grass seed
- four paper cups
- potting soil
- fertilizer for grass or plants
- spoon
- water
- metric ruler

🔄 Procedure

Have an adult prepare the fertilizer according to package directions. Label the paper cups as follows: A—water only, B—3mL fertilizer, C—5 mL fertilizer, D—10 mL fertilizer. Fill each cup half-full with soil. Sprinkle 5 mL of grass seed into each cup. Initially give each cup 20 mL of water. Place the cups on a windowsill or other appropriate location. The next day and everyday thereafter give each cup 5 mL of water.

After one week, many of the seeds should have sprouted, and you may begin the experiment. Measure the height (in centimeters) of the tallest blade of grass in each cup and record the heights under Day 1 on the data sheet. Be sure to write the measurement in the correct place. Give each cup the 5 mL of water you have been giving them everyday. Also give the cup labeled A a 3 mL portion of fertilizer. Give the cup labeled B a 5 mL portion of fertilizer. Give the cup labeled C a 10 mL portion of fertilizer.

On Day 2, measure the height of the tallest blade of grass in each cup. Record the heights in the proper columns of the data sheet. Again give each cup 15 mL of water and the amount of fertilizer indicated on the cup. On Day 3, measure the height of the tallest blade of grass, then water and fertilize the grass. Continue with this procedure for 10 days.

The control group is the grass cup receiving water only. Grass may grow the same with or without fertilizer. The variables are controlled by giving each grass cup the same amount of water; placing them in the same place so that they receive the same amount of light and heat; and using the same potting soil, seed type, and fertilizer. The only difference should be the amount of fertilizer given each cup.

© McGraw-Hill Children's Publishing   IF19216 Building Science Skills

Student lab sheet

Individual/Small Group Experiment

Name: _____ Date: _____

What Is the Effect of Fertilizer on Grass Growth?
(Page 2 of 2)

Graph the results and complete the Student Lab Sheet.

Data

The Effect of Fertilizer on Grass Growth

		Water Only	3 mL Fertilizer	5 mL Fertilizer	10 mL Fertilizer
Height in Centimeters (cm)	Day 1				
	Day 2				
	Day 3				
	Day 4				
	Day 5				
	Day 6				
	Day 7				
	Day 8				
	Day 9				
	Day 10				

Student lab sheet

Individual/Small Group Experiment

Name: _____ Date: _____

What Is the Effect of Music on Memory?
(Page 1 of 3)

 **Question**

What is the effect of music on memory?

 **Materials**

- 20 small objects
- tray and a piece of newspaper
- audiotape or CD of classical music
- audiotape or CD of contemporary music
- CD/audiotape player
- paper and pencils
- clock/timer
- five or more test subjects

Procedure

Write down the names of 10 objects you select from the 20 you gathered. Place them on the tray and cover with the newspaper. Do not let your subjects see what is on the tray. Place the tray in the middle of a table. Have the subjects sit at the table. Read these directions:

"In a minute I will uncover this tray. On it you will see 10 objects. Your job is to try to memorize as many of these objects as you can in one minute. After one minute I will remove the tray, give you a sheet of paper and a pencil, and give you one minute to write down the names of the objects. Any questions?"

Look at your start time and remove the newspaper. After one minute, say "stop" and remove the tray. Cover it with the newspaper so no on will see the objects.

Pass out paper and pencils. Look at the start time and tell everyone to begin writing down the names of the objects they remember. After one minute, announce "stop" and collect the papers. Label the papers "no music" and place them aside along with your list of objects that were on that tray. Later you will add up the number of objects each person correctly identified.

© McGraw-Hill Children's Publishing — IF19216 *Building Science Skills*

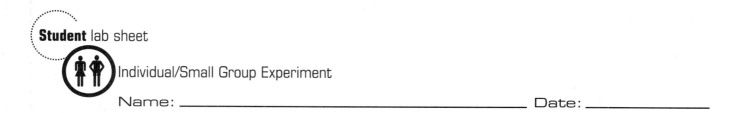

What Is the Effect of Music on Memory?
(Page 2 of 3)

Have the CD/tape player ready with the classical or contemporary music. Repeat the experiment with another tray of ten objects (three or four may be the same objects as the first time). Be sure to write down the names of the objects on the tray before you begin. This time, before you uncover the tray, start playing the music.

After one minute, remove the tray and cover up the objects. Pass out paper. Once again look at the start time and tell the subjects to write down the names of the objects they can remember. Be sure to continue playing the music while people are thinking and writing. After one minute, stop the music, collect the papers, and label them with the music type.

For the third test, have the CD/tape player ready with the other music selection. Repeat the experiment in the same way but show a different set of 10 objects on the tray. When everyone is finished, collect their papers and label them with the music type.

Now it is time to look at your data. Correct each paper. Write the number of correctly named objects on each paper and on the data chart below. When making a graph you may use either the total number of correct answers from all the subjects added together or calculate the average number of correct answers for each music type and for no music.

In this experiment, the control group is the "no background music" memory test. The main variables being controlled are the way memory is tested and the people participating. If different people were used each time, some may have better memories than others.

Complete a graph and the Student Lab Sheet.

Student lab sheet

Individual/Small Group Experiment

Name: _____ Date: _____

What Is the Effect of Music on Memory?
(Page 3 of 3)

 Data

	No Music	Classical Music	Popular Music	Subject Comments
Subject 1				
Subject 2				
Subject 3				
Subject 4				
Subject 5				
Total Correct				
Average Correct				

Student lab sheet

Individual/Small Group Experiment

Name: _____ Date: _____

How Does Exercise Affect Lung Capacity?

❓ Question

How does exercise affect lung capacity?

📦 Materials

- table tennis ball
- long table
- meter stick
- test subject

🔲 Procedure

Have the subject stand at the end of the long table. Set the table tennis ball as close to the edge of the table as possible. The subject should take a deep breath and blow the ball across the table with just the one breath and without moving forward. When the ball comes to a stop, measure the distance it traveled in centimeters. Record the distance in the chart below.

Next have the subject do 25 jumping jacks. While the subject is exercising, reposition the ball. Immediately after exercising, have the subject take a deep breath and blow the ball across the table. Measure the distance the ball traveled and record the results.

Repeat once more, this time having the subject do an additional 25 jumping jacks. Measure the distance the ball traveled and record the results.

If the subject is able to blow the ball off the table, use the floor. Mark a starting line with masking tape, have the subject lay on the floor behind the line and blow the ball. Measure the distance just as above.

If desired, repeat the experiment with additional subjects and compare the results.

📄 Data

	No Exercise	After 25 Jumping Jacks	After 50 Total Jumping Jacks
Distance the Table Tennis Ball Traveled			

© McGraw-Hill Children's Publishing

IF19216 Building Science Skills

Assessment Rubric

	4	3	2	1
Conducting the Experiment	Great deal of attention to detail; followed procedure carefully; effort shown to control variables; cleaned up	Good deal of attention to detail; followed procedure with minimal need for corrections; shows effort to control variables; good clean up effort	Needed to redo steps in the procedure due to carelessness; trouble following directions; some awareness of controlling variables; fair clean up effort	Little effort in following procedure; poor use of materials; poor clean up
Graphs and Charts	Accurate, neat, color used effectively; data depicted clearly; easy to read	Minor errors that do not affect data; neat and fairly easy to read	Some errors in depicting the data; sloppy; takes effort to read	Data not accurately depicted; messy and confusing
Conclusion and Discussion	High level of logical reasoning; expanded ideas; thoughtful responses; accurate interpretations	Effort shown in expanding ideas; logical interpretations; thoughtful responses	Short responses; little effort shown in expanded thought; inaccurate interpretations	Incomplete responses; illogical; little effort shown
Quality of Lab Write-up	Great deal of effort shown; neat; complete sentences, no spelling errors; good grammar	Good deal of effort shown; neat; very few spelling errors; complete sentences	Messy; spelling errors; incomplete sentences	Messy; illegible; not complete; many errors

© McGraw-Hill Children's Publishing 70 IF19216 *Building Science Skills*

Culminating Event—A Science Fair

A science fair is a wonderful opportunity for students not only to conduct an experiment but to proudly display their work. A science fair can be set up in the classroom or open area where tables are available, such as the cafeteria or gymnasium. Each student creates an experiment, conducts it, and makes a display that contains his/her experiment write up and, if appropriate, the components of the experiment itself. Invitations are given to parents and other classes to view the displays and to speak with the student scientists about their projects. At many science fairs projects are judged and ribbons are awarded for outstanding work.

When organizing a science fair, begin planning about two months in advance. The checklist on page 72 highlights major components of a science fair. It outlines what needs to be done for a science fair that is judged and has invited guests. A smaller scale science fair is certainly less involved and easier to organize and manage. Support students in designing their experiments. A listing of possible experiments can be found on pages 76–77. Approve all experiments before students begin. Students can complete the Student Lab Sheets through the procedure section, hand it in for your approval, and then actually conduct the experiment. The Science Fair Investigation Checklist (page 74) and Science Fair Display Checklist (page 75) can be used to help students stay on track and to provide additional guidelines and structure to their efforts. Experiments may be conducted at home to alleviate time, space, and material constraints. Those conducting experiments with plants/seeds need to allow plenty of time for growth and changes. Students can also complete the display at home using the guidelines on page 75. Be sure to read the guidelines in advance and make any changes necessary for your specific fair.

The judging procedure used here does not have students competing against each other. All students can earn first place ribbons if the quality of their experiments and displays deserves it. A rubric is used to critique the students' projects. Give the rubric, found on page 78, to the students in advance. Explain exactly what is needed to earn the full amount of points in each category. Students, individually, make the choice to put the effort into earning a high score or not.

If you decide to have judges, select two or more to insure consistency in judging. Each project is, therefore, looked at, read, and scored by more than one person. Ideally, give the judges the rubric in advance of the fair. If a large number of projects are being judged (over 50), invite more people to act as judges, but have each project scored by at least two judges. High school science students often make excellent judges. Judging should take place before the fair actually opens to guests so that ribbons can be awarded and displayed during the fair.

A science fair need not be a large formal event. It can easily be a small classroom special project. The most important thing is that the students are involved in this scientific process, exhibit pride in this hands-on activity, and share their pride and learning with others.

Culminating event
Science Fair

Planning Checklist for Teacher

	✓	Date Completed
Date Selected		
Location chosen and reserved		
Tables/desks available		
Judges recruited		
Judges sent guidelines and rubric		
Invitations made		
Invitations sent out		
Confirm judges		
Token gift for judges purchased		
Certificates and ribbons purchased or made		
Science Fair concept introduced to students		
Assign students to design an experiment. Hand out Experiment Possibilities as a source of ideas.		
Experiment questions approved		
Materials and procedure approved; sections completed on Student Lab Sheet		
Assign due date for completing actual experiment and remainder of Student Lab Sheet.		
Create a model of an experiment display.		
Review with students guidelines and judging rubric for display.		
Hand out guidelines and judging rubric.		
Establish procedure for bringing in and setting up displays.		

Student lab sheet

Individual/Small Group Experiment

Name: _____ Date: _____

Guidelines for Science Fair Display

- Three-panel displays are the most common type of display because they are freestanding and information can be organized easily.
- The display should be durable. Foam board works well, as does cardboard.
- Space may be limited. A good size for a display is 30 inches by 40 inches (76 cm x 102 cm).
- The display should include the student's name, title, question, materials list, procedure, data, graphs, results, conclusion, and discussion.
- Make the title large, neat, and clear.
- Use color, being careful not to use distracting patterns or designs.
- Information may be prepared on a computer or handwritten. It should be neat with few or no errors.
- Sketch with a pencil first before using marker, paints, or pen. Mistakes are easier to erase when made with pencil.
- Arrange papers first before gluing them in place.
- Parts of your experiment may be set on the table/desk in front of your display. This helps with the understanding of your experiment and makes your display more appealing.
- No experiment should involve harmful bacteria or dangerous chemicals.
- No experiment should cause the pain or suffering of any animal, including humans.
- No experiment should involve highly flammable materials (bathroom cleaners, etc.).
- No display should include medicines, drugs, tobacco, or alcohol.
- Expensive or fragile items should not be displayed. Use photos, drawings, or models.

Name: _____   Date: _____

Science Fair Investigation Checklist

	Date Due	Date Completed	Teacher's Initials
Experimental Question			
Procedures and Materials List Written			
Materials Gathered			
Actual Experiment Conducted			
Student Lab Sheet Complete			
Display Finished			
Bring Display in for Science Fair			

Culminating event
Science Fair
Name: _____ Date: _____

Science Fair Display Checklist

	✓ if great	✓ if ok	✓ if changes are needed	changes to be made
Display is neat, freestanding, and interesting to view.				
Name on display, title, question, materials list, procedure, data, results, conclusions, and discussion				
Was the scientific method used? Is there evidence of controlled variables?				
Does the procedure make sense? Is all information correct?				
Are data, graphics, and charts neat and clear? Are metric measurements made?				
Does the conclusion answer the original question?				
Is the discussion thoughtful? Does it include what you learned, other experiment ideas, improvements?				
Are sentences complete? Did you check for spelling errors?				
How much effort did you put into this display? Do parts look rushed?				
Have someone read over your experiment display. Make final changes.				

© McGraw-Hill Children's Publishing — IF19216 *Building Science Skills*

Culminating event
Science Fair

Name: _____ Date: _____

Experiment Possibilities

Life Science
- How does yeast type affect how dough rises?
- How does sugar type affect how dough rises?
- How does body size affect lung capacity?
- How does music affect plant growth?
- How does colored light affect plant growth?
- How does acid affect plant growth?
- How does temperature affect seeds?
- How does food coloring affect food preference?
- How does caffeine affect heart rate?
- How does exercise affect heart rate?
- How does exercise affect breathing rate?
- What is the effect of temperature on mold growth?
- What is the effect of light on mold growth?
- What is the effect of color on food preference in animals?
- Do gerbils/hamsters recognize color?
- What is the effect of time limits on completing/learning a task?

Physical Science
Chemistry
- How does moisture affect the size of popped popcorn?
- How does a specific ingredient affect a baked good?
- How does salt affect rust rate?
- Does car wax slow the rate of rusting?
- How does moisture level affect rust rate?
- How does metal type affect rust rate?
- How does moisture affect paper biodegradability?
- How does water temperature affect stain removal?
- What is the effect of milk fat on glue making?
- What is the effect of bleach on fabric strength?
- How do various substances affect the pH levels in soil?

© McGraw-Hill Children's Publishing   76   IF19216 Building Science Skills

Culminating event
Science Fair

Name: _____ Date: _____

Experiment Possibilities

Physics
- How does temperature affect drying rate?
- How is drying rate affected by wind speed?
- How does fabric type affect temperature?
- How does ice shape affect melting rate?
- How does container shape affect freezing rate?
- How does salt affect freezing rates?
- How does temperature affect dough rising?
- Does stretching a balloon make it easier to blow up?
- How does rubber band thickness affect elasticity?
- How does substance (concrete, wood, etc.) affect heat absorption?
- Does the light bulb wattage affect heat output?
- How does thickness of wood affect insulation value?
- Does wood type affect insulation value?
- How does length of string affect pendulum swing rate?
- How does pendulum weight affect swing rate?
- How does weight affect drop rate?
- How does shape affect drop rate through water?
- How does the number of coils on an electromagnet affect level of magnetism?
- How does nail size affect level of electromagnetic strength?
- How does floor surface affect friction?
- How does paper towel type affect absorption rate?
- How does paper towel thickness affect absorption rate?
- How does temperature affect crystal growth?
- How does ball size affect bounce height?

© McGraw-Hill Children's Publishing   IF19216 Building Science Skills

Culminating event

Science Fair **Judging Rubric**

Student's name: _____

Title of Project: _____

Circle score next to each category
10 being the highest

#	Category	Score
1.	**Exhibit — General Appearance** (Display is neat, freestanding, and interesting to view.)	1 2 3 4 5 6 7 8 9 10
2.	**Exhibit — General Content** (Display has all the essential components: student's name, title, question, materials list, procedure, data, results, conclusion, and discussion.)	1 2 3 4 5 6 7 8 9 10
3.	Scientific Method (Was the scientific method used? Is there evidence of variables being controlled?)	1 2 3 4 5 6 7 8 9 10
4.	Procedure (Is the procedure in a logical sequence? Could this experiment be repeated by someone else following this procedure?)	1 2 3 4 5 6 7 8 9 10
5.	Data, Graphs, and Charts (Were measurements accurately taken? Metric units used? Are graphs accurate?)	1 2 3 4 5 6 7 8 9 10
6.	Conclusions (Are conclusions logical? Valid?)	1 2 3 4 5 6 7 8 9 10
7.	Discussion (Is the discussion thoughtful, reflecting knowledge gained, improvements, problems?)	1 2 3 4 5 6 7 8 9 10
8.	Written Work (Are sentences complete? Minimum number of spelling and grammatical errors?)	1 2 3 4 5 6 7 8 9 10
9.	Effort (Degree of individual effort demonstrated)	1 2 3 4 5 6 7 8 9 10
10.	Creativity and Originality (Does project show creativity in thought and design?)	1 2 3 4 5 6 7 8 9 10

Comments:
_____
_____
_____
_____
_____

Total Score: _____

_____
Judge's signature

Awards (totaled from two judges):
First   171–200
Second   141–170
Third   111–140
Certificate   All

Participation Award for the Science Fair

Given to

_____

for

_____

Proudly presented this _____ day of _____

Signed _____

Science Fair

© McGraw-Hill Children's Publishing   IF19216 *Building Science Skills*

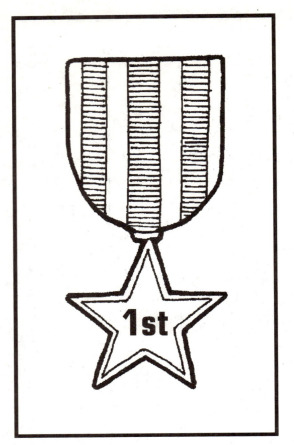
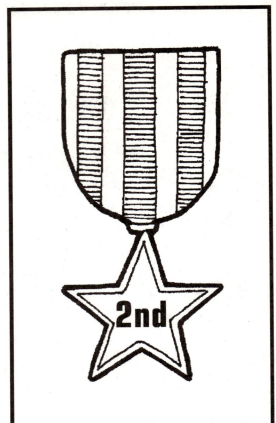
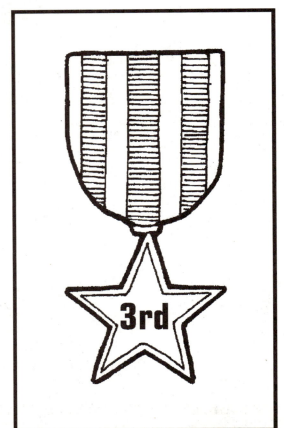